Living Peace Philosophy

An Introduction

By Alaric Hutchinson

LIVING PEACE PHILOSOPHY: AN INTRODUCTION Copyright © 2017 by Alaric Kyle Hutchinson. Earth Spirit Publishing, LLC, Queen Creek, AZ. All rights reserved. No part of this book may be used or produced in any manner whatsoever without written permission, except in the case of brief quotations embodied in critical articles and reviews. For information, contact the publisher at:
www.earthspiritcenter.org

ISBN: 978-0-9904058-5-6

Dedication

I do not grasp
Nor hold onto.
I release and
Set all things free.

This book is dedicated to the seekers of peace.
May you find within what you have been searching for without.

One day you will awaken,
Laughing out loud, and
By sitting, doing nothing,
You will understand.

An Invitation

What you hold in your hands is an introduction to the philosophy and psychology of my life's work that came to be in 2014 through my first book, *Living Peace*. The first in what is to be an expansive, seven-book series, *Living Peace* and its teachings provide a solid foundation upon which an individual can build a joyful, loving, and peaceful life. It is more than "self-help" and more than an idealistic philosophy. What you will find in these pages is practical insight into human behavior and the collective way of thinking that we as a species all take part in. By understanding our psychology, we gain the ability to choose another course of action that heals all emotional wounds and fosters inner peace. We may then respond to the conflicts of life with understanding and compassion, as opposed to creating more pain when we feel offended or threatened and react impulsively.

For now, let us reflect on the Living Peace Code. Before you venture any further, I invite you to turn to page 1 and read the code. Let its message sink in then read it again. It is what holds these teachings together. Reading the Code daily—or even committing it to memory and reciting it daily—will be of great service to you. In times when we lose our peace by becoming upset, which then leads to the mistreatment of ourselves and others, we can always come back to the Code for a gentle yet firm reminder that we hold the power within our hands to refocus our awareness and be the masters of our lives.

Table of Contents

Dedication iii

An Invitation iv

The Living Peace Code 1

Mastery of Thought 3

Mastery of Impulse 7

Mastery of Emotion 11

Ignorance is Illusion; *We Seek Understanding* 15

Chaos is Illusion; *We Seek Harmony* 19

Duality is Illusion; *We Seek Transcendence* 23

Release the Mundane 27

Release Knowing 31

Release Self 35

Visit with Me 38

The Living Peace Code

P.E.A.C.E.
People Embracing **A** Conscious Evolution

I **AM** the Master of my Life:
I Master my Thoughts.
I Master my Impulses.
I Master my Emotions.

I see **THROUGH** Illusion:
There is no Ignorance.
There is no Chaos.
There is no Duality.

I Forever **SEEK** and Cultivate:
Understanding,
Harmony, and,
Transcendence.

Everything is Impermanent. Change is the only Constant.

I RELEASE my Attachments to the Mundane World.
I RELEASE my Attachments to What I Know.
I RELEASE my Attachments to Who I Am.
I RELINQUISH… **My SELF**…

I **AM**
P.E.A.C.E.
People Embodying **A** Conscious Evolution

Alaric Hutchinson, author
Excerpted from his book, *Living Peace*

Living Peace Philosophy: an Invitation

Tenet One

Mastery of Thought

Thought is the building block of reality;
Therefore, our lives are mirrors of our minds.
Thoughts are opinions and perceptions—not facts.
To transform reality, we must first change our thoughts.

Why is thought the building block of reality? Take a step outside and look around—our entire civilization is the byproduct of thought, including the directions societies take due to cultural, political, and religious thinking. We forget this. We forget that all forward progress stems from ideas and the people who followed through with those ideas. Our world and its challenges today look the way they do not because this is the only way the world can be, but because it reflects the current extent of our combined human level of consciousness.

On a micro level, the same also applies when we sit and contemplate our individual existence and life choices. The lives we have created today have all stemmed from the thoughts, ideas, and beliefs we have consciously or unconsciously agreed to. They have heavily influenced every choice we've made and will make. The stories we believe—and repeatedly tell—have a major impact on the amount of self-worth, confidence, and willingness to be open with others that we possess. When we get hurt, we close ourselves off and begin missing out on everyday opportunities for growth and expansion. Then when opportunities for love or success come knocking, we hide behind the door and refuse to open it. We may then say that the world is an unloving or unfair place, all the while forgetting it was our choice to close ourselves off because once upon a time, in a time that no longer exists except as a figment of our imagination, we felt hurt.

The amount of fear or trust we have in life has to do with our perceptions and the projected perceptions of our parents that we may have been under the influence of while growing up. However, we cannot blame those who raised us for they were simply byproducts of their parents' perceptions and the perceptions of the collective society at the time, and so on clear back to the beginning of humankind. The one thing we do have power over is our ability to "wake up" and become intentional thinkers.

Life is a mirror because, as humans, we have the uncanny ability to see only what we want to see, or only see what we expect to see. Due to our individual biases, desires, life experiences, and assumptive thinking, ten people can experience the same situation but each one will walk away with a completely different perception of what occurred and his or her unique story concerning it. The facts are the basis of what happened, but we never stop at the facts—instead we add our opinions as to the whys and the hows of what occurred. We weave our fictional stories around the facts.

This is quite pertinent when meeting a new person who seems overly quiet and potentially uninterested in us, making it easy to walk away from the experience believing any number of things (normally negative) about the person— or us. Someone with an untrained mind might project their own story of insecurity onto the person, believing that the person disliked and rejected them, while someone with high confidence wouldn't even think such a thought, but might instead consider that the person might have had a hard day, thus fostering compassion rather than insecurity about the meeting.

In Mastery of Thought, we learn to not add assumptive stories to our experiences. In the above example we would simply stop at observing that the person was "quiet" and not spend time guessing why. Unless we ask the person the next time we see them what the cause of their "quietness" was, any pondering is pure illusion-making.

Life as a mirror can be dangerous or beautiful, because when we operate predominantly in a negative or positive mode, we can't help but filter everything we experience through one lens or the other. Everything reflects our own positivity or negativity. When we are unaware of this, life can be very painful, but when we become aware, we learn how to shift our thoughts and our story-telling to create more acceptance of others and peace in our own hearts.

People have very real physical symptoms stemming from emotions based on the thoughts they think, whether or not what they are thinking is actually true or even exists.

Understanding Illusion:

This is the realization that what we think is illusory, especially when we explore memory, future projections, or assumptive story-telling.

Understanding Belief:

Beliefs are fixed perceptions that consistently hue our realities until we become aware of them and intentionally change them.

Tenet Two
Mastery of Impulse

The wise never react,
For reaction is reserved for the blind.
Breath brings pause that allows response to occur.
By responding, the wise create reality.

It is important to note that "the blind" refers to a figurative blindness. In this book, the term represents individuals who are unaware, while "the wise" represents individuals who have awakened their human potential and now see beyond the ego.

Continuing to build on top of the last tenet, impulse control—or rather impulse awareness—is of the utmost importance when it comes to catching one's thoughts before they turn into regrettable words, actions, or life-altering decisions.

Humans have the tendency to react when stimulated by some outside force, often feeling "triggered" (frightened, hurt, insulted, disrespected, etc.). Now that we are aware that what we think and feel is not necessarily true, this understanding helps us cool the fires of our impulsiveness when interacting with others. The ability to be introspective is not something the blind possess, and that is what keeps them trapped in their negative emotional continuums. On the other hand, the wise continuously reflect on why they feel the way they do, and where these feelings come from (within themselves).

It is never of benefit to react with "knee-jerk" impulse because such a reaction is always a temporary uprising that often later leads to expanded forms of negative feelings such as guilt or shame if a highly emotional reaction occurred. By catching our impulsive tendencies—choosing to consciously shift them so that we speak from a place of peace, reason, and compassion—we break the cycle and begin to create a different reality for ourselves, free from unconsciously reproducing the same problems for ourselves day after day.

Mastery of Impulse is also relevant when it comes to addictive tendencies. Negative reaction is indeed a form of addiction, possibly the greatest addiction humans have, but let us explore the other external addictions more deeply. The root of most addictions stems from a desire to escape pain or one's reality of perceived constant suffering. What starts off as a way to escape our pain and bring relief eventually becomes the very activity that traps us in our suffering. Without acknowledging and embracing what is causing us pain, we cannot learn from it or transform it. We continue to impulsively avoid what bothers us.

The wise are able to create and change their reality because they allow room for pause in their life. Most addictions tend to flare up during times of aloneness because subconscious, painful thoughts and memories surface when there is no external stimulation to distract from them. The blind continue to avoid these moments, while the wise use this time, no matter how painful it may be, to explore their minds and turn their suffering into useful information. This information then becomes fertilizer to help them grow.

Later tenets will expand upon this idea, but it was important to point out why we avoid the things that will help us the most, like the practice of simply sitting with ourselves and taking a good look at what's going on inside. This becomes easier and easier to do as we learn that pain is not bad, nor is it an enemy. Pain is necessary for our conscious growth, and when we embrace it, we start the process of healing our emotional impulsiveness, mental and physical reactions, and physical addictions.

Sometimes people feel the need to react or yell in anger because their calm speech falls on deaf ears—but they must ask themselves, what results do anger bring? Anger may motivate, but it also kills inspiration. It is important to understand that it is not enough to simply speak calmly; we must also practice compassionate listening and the freedom to disagree without interruption.

Understanding Pause:

Intentional breathing creates pause, which can be used as an anchor for mindfulness anytime and anywhere.

Understanding Response:

By changing the way in which we respond to life, all of life itself begins to respond differently to us.

Tenet Three
Mastery of Emotion

Like the ocean, emotions ebb and flow,
Like the sun, emotions bring us sight.
Neither wrong nor right, emotion is but information,
Illuminating ego and teaching impermanence.

This cannot be repeated enough: **just because we think a thought or feel an emotion doesn't automatically make it true!** When we take a step back from our emotions, applying Mastery of Thought and Impulse, we unleash the ability of Unattachment. Our emotional suffering stems from resisting reality and a holding onto what we wish could have been or our judgment of what should have been. In other words, our peace begins when we release all hope of having a better past!

Negative self-certainty is a trap many of us fall into when we become upset. It can also be the very reason we become upset. Letting go involves letting go of our certainty about ourselves, about others, and about how life should be. There truly are not "shoulds" in life because in each present moment there is only ever what is or what isn't. Understanding this helps us remain unattached and at peace with things, because emotions are then broken down into an understanding that, "I am either resisting what is, or I am accepting what is". All negative emotion arises from resisting the situations and circumstances of life as they are.

Unattachment is caring deeply about someone or something, yet not letting this concern influence our emotional well being. When we become emotional, we realize that we are attached, hooked, or possibly codependent, requiring someone or something outside of ourselves to satisfy our emotional needs. This way of living will always lead to suffering because everything is impermanent; everything is temporary. We forget this, expect things and people to remain the same (provide for us, stay alive for us) and that is why we suffer. Pain happens yes, especially during times of loss, but those times are fleeting, and life continues on. Suffering only continues when we hold onto people, things, and our stories of grief. Holding on keeps us living in illusion, unable to see the miracle of life still present around us each and every day.

Emotions are simply information. Being upset is a signal that we are temporarily stuck in ego and buying stock in an illusion. Negative emotions show us where we may place attention within ourselves to cultivate greater peace, harmony, and overall healing.

When we are irritated by another, it is an opportunity to develop our compassion and self-understanding as to why we feel threatened or why we feel bothered. In truth, the vast majority of the time there is no real threat, so we must override the part of our brain that wants to go to battle. "I am safe here, and all is well." is a wonderful affirmation to repeat during times of emotional triggering, especially at work or during difficult but necessary conversations with loved ones. When we can learn to surf the waves of our emotions instead of being beaten up and drowned by them, we then gain the ability to be more present for others. We can then foster not only peace but we will also find greater enjoyment in the lives of those we engage with.

Never deny or avoid an emotion you are feeling. To be in denial is to ignore the information necessary for your conscious growth.

Understanding Forgiveness:

Rather than focusing on forgiveness, learn to accept, because the moment we accept something, we let it go, and there is nothing left to forgive.

Understanding Unattachment:

Honor each person's path and story without taking them home and then to bed with you.

Tenet Four

Ignorance is Illusion;
We Seek Understanding

Ignorance is a chosen state of mind,
Limiting the beautiful view of self and others.
Compassion dissolves ignorance,
Allowing sight of the splendor and purpose in All.

When we choose to stop listening or attempting to understand those we are in conflict with, be it loved ones or strangers, we enter into the realm of ignorance. The realm of ignorance is a chosen state of being in which we close our minds to learning anything new or accepting anything more. Often, we enter into this state due to insecurity, fear, a wounded ego, or by self-justification, certain we are right. When issues, people, or the world as a collective seems easily split into right OR wrong, or good OR bad, it is very easy to remain ignorantly blissful. However, the world is not black OR white but is living multicolor. Thus, our judgments that keep us separate from everything that makes us uncomfortable also keep us trapped in our pride, our pity, our anger, and our grief. Inner peace being our new goal, it takes time and patience to explore the root of our judgments of self and others. By exploring and having curious minds, we begin to realize that everything holds purpose and everyone has worth.

"Everyone is doing the best they can with what they know." is a wonderful way of looking at life. This acknowledgement provides room for compassion to grow in our hearts—towards ourselves and others. The reason compassion dissolves ignorance is because when we have compassion for others, even when they are projecting their pain onto us, we don't write them off or judge them. We simply sit, listen, hold space, and wait. Sometimes that, in and of itself, is healing, while other times it creates a space of receptivity so that, once the person feels complete in their expression, we may then engage them in a more compassionate conversation. Because they were heard and fully allowed to emote without our impulsive interruptions, the road is paved for them to hear us out in turn, allowing a bridge of understanding to be built.

As mentioned earlier in Mastery of Emotion, realizing "there is no threat here" is a major point of awareness to focus upon. It also applies to this tenet because when we feel threatened, we shut ourselves down, or try to shut the other person down. When we truly make disagreement something that is "okay", we instantly remove the "threat" trigger, allowing more honest and open communication to occur. When people are afraid of upsetting others, they simply do not communicate fully or else they tend to sugarcoat the truth, which leads to people-pleasing, another obstacle to growth.

Belittling and sugarcoating are flipsides of the same coin of dishonesty. Neither looks at or treats life with neutrality. Without this unbiased, neutral approach, genuine understanding remains hidden beneath layers of sweet lies or joking self-degradation.

Understanding Acceptance:

We don't need to have an opinion about everyone and everything; instead we can simply accept the realities that other people choose.

Understanding Compassion:

There is no pity in compassion, as compassion is an exchange between equals.

Tenet Five

Chaos is Illusion;
We seek Harmony

Chaos is a word used by the uninitiated mind.
Harmony is seen in All by the practiced mind.
Peace may be found amidst any storm,
For the blossom is kin to the thorn.

We continue our journey toward releasing judgment, furthering our knowledge and understanding of the world as we peer into chaos. Objectivity is a necessity as we explore this realm of thought; else we ourselves may become part of the maelstrom. In truth, our minds are the source of most of the chaos we experience in our lives. The stress or drama we feel on a daily basis exists only because of our skewed perceptions of the world and our experiences in it. Chaos, like stress, cannot exist unless our thoughts are in agreement with it or our words and actions are feeding it. In times that seem chaotic and groundless, we grab at anything we can for support and hold tight, which often makes things much worse. This goes back to the survival "flight or fight" reactive behavior that we must intentionally override within our minds to instead choose a course of rational thought and peace.

A brilliant example of this is when a loved one asks for space. Our reaction is to cling tighter out of fear of losing our connection with them. In not providing the requested spacious freedom, we create the very thing we fear. By resisting their desire, we create chaos due to our own insecurities and the need to feel secure at all times. When they resist, or simply cannot meet our desire, the relationship becomes stressed to the point of collapse. Paradoxically, chaos becomes a nonissue when we find comfort in groundlessness and the unknown. After all, the truer truth is that everything is impermanent. Thus any sense of security and groundedness is temporary and, in some aspect, an illusion. Accepting this fact eventually brings a sense of inner peace.

Accepting that "the blossom is kin to the thorn" introduces a non-dualistic approach to life. This begins the process of learning how to find peace amidst any storm. In nature, there is no "good OR bad" or "right OR wrong". Everything has its place and purpose, and all things are necessary to sustain life. Think of a rose... We love the scent and sight of the beautiful flower, but we disdain its painful thorn. We might be inclined to call the thorn "bad" or wish the rose to be other than what it is, thorn-less, but the rose would not remain so beauteous without the protection of its thorns. All things have a right to existence. All things have purpose. Our desire that this be different is pure projection and self-absorption. And we do this to people all the time, asking them to be different and other than what they uniquely and beautifully are.

It is of vital importance we learn the art of allowing all life, including other people to "just be". Throughout history tampering with cultures and ecosystems has caused much harm. In the microcosm, we can see how tampering with the lives of our loved ones can actually push them further into addiction and feelings of separation. In fact, "tampering" might be seen as another word for "judgment". We feel that we are right and "justified" in meddling, forgetting that it is our job to listen, understand, and hold space for them—not to be their savior. In other words, we must learn to allow all things to grow in their own time. Tender care is possible without judgment and tampering, and when we care for ourselves and others with patience and mindfulness, harmony is found, much like that which exists in nature. People are not weeds to be pulled, nor are their unsightly qualities meant to be ripped out. Trying to force change only leads to further chaos. Instead, we allow, we watch, and we offer support—and with this peaceful approach, we begin to notice that each person bears a unique and beautiful blossom of their own. We also see that not everyone will be nourished the same in the same soil.

When caught in the rapids of a river, sometimes it is better to let go and flow downstream to where the waters have calmed, rather than griping tight to a stationary rock or branch and remaining in the chaotic currents.

Understanding Objectivity:

Good intentions can cause much harm, thus we learn not to pity or judge; we simply observe with neutrality and act accordingly without an agenda of our own.

Understanding Allowing:

In our haste we become blinded and create chaos in our wake. There is no rush, for peace never hurries.

Tenet Six

Duality is Illusion;
We seek Transcendence

Duality is the judgment of perceived opposites.
All opposites are the same and may be reconciled.
Paradox paves the way for enlightenment, for
Conflict ceases when discrimination ceases.

Let's keep building upon the previous tenet's approach to non-duality. In order to fully understand the concept of "duality", we must first understand "polarity". Polarity is the dual nature of reality, meaning that everything has extremes and poles—north and south, hot and cold, hard and soft. Duality is the *addition* of psychological and philosophical poles that are human-made by the ego, such as right OR wrong, good OR bad, and even the extremes of hate in opposition to love or fear in opposition to trust. Polarity is neutral, but the duality we *add* to opposites in our everyday lives creates much suffering because we use it to discriminate against anything "different" and reinforce our stories of conflict.

In transcendence (rising above), we seek to honor the polarity of life, while ceasing our discrimination against it. Balance is necessary in order for things to thrive, thus everything has masculine and feminine principles—or rather, giving and receiving principles. Unless both work in harmony, the balance is disturbed and pain ensues.

We must learn to be strong yet flexible, confident yet humble, and logical yet intuitive. These seemingly opposite qualities actually exist on the same pole of experience and vary only in degree. We seek the equilibrium of both, while transcending the discriminating mind that chooses one over the other. Discriminating manifests itself as imbalance in our lives. For example, the polarity of wellbeing and pain is very active and unavoidable, yet we resist it at all costs, nonetheless. In our misguided efforts to avoid pain, we activate it to such a degree that it becomes suffering. Multitudes live for years in unhappiness because they have no awareness of the need to reconcile these two seeming opposites. Nor do they realize that in order for wellness to ensue, their pain must first be embraced and accepted.

We see this avoidance in the way people shun the death experience, and in how the beauty industry flourishes because so many are desperately grasping at anything that might help them remain youthful forever. The more we try to avoid the natural process of aging and pretend that death will never come, the more we will experience fear and suffering because of it. Only by embracing the impermanence of life and the normal deteriorating effects of time will we gain time's wisdom and the ability to live more presently and joyously. The running stops, and so does the chase, and the idea that we are whole right here, right now is introduced. The reconciliation of opposites occurs when we realize that both are needed for wholeness to be actualized.

By realizing duality is an illusion, we realize that life is more about "This AND Thats" rather than "This OR Thats". Transcending the dualistic thinking of right OR wrong and good OR bad, we eventually transcend judgment altogether. By rising above judgment, we are one step closer to becoming the embodiment of peace and being fully present for our loved ones. At this point, conflict becomes much less of an issue, yet there is still the challenge of ego and attachment to the things and people we love which causes us pain. These, we will remedy in the final three tenets.

Without opposites, there is nothing left to compare, so all expectation is dropped and peace is maintained.

Understanding Reconciliation:

Without right OR wrong, our new guidance system becomes the choice of what creates peace over what creates pain.

Understanding Transcendence:

When we rise above conflict and gain a broader perspective, we can't help but find the humor in our daily "struggle". We see that it's "silly" to fight so hard against the inevitability of impermanence or to lose our peace over the most trivial matters.

Tenet Seven

Release the Mundane

There is nothing more to grasp or gain;
Everything fades, yet everything remains.
Wholeness is present from the moment of birth,
Yet the blind find lack where the wise see worth.

Releasing the mundane occurs when we realize that everything is always well, even when it does not appear to be. From the ego's perspective, there is always something more to do and something more to gain. Yet the more we step back from our egos, becoming the observers behind our minds, we realize that these ideas do not actually have their roots in absolute truth. They exist because we make them exist. Yes, we need to eat, sleep, and provide a shelter over our heads—but the need to have or be anything beyond that is a myth that our cultures have chosen as a collective to buy stock in. On a macro level, we *are* capable of changing society. On a micro level, we *are* capable of changing our everyday lives and removing the enormous pressure we place upon ourselves to be perfect or something other than or more than what we are.

A common trait among many people who find themselves stuck in negative thinking is that there is an overemphasis on what's not working in their lives. They then use these critical examples to reinforce their lack, victimhood, and stories of un-lovability. Collectively, it is the holding onto these negative stories and ideas about one's self and others that perpetuates feelings of lack, brokenness, incompleteness, and un-wholeness. This can be traced back to negative self-certainty. Rather than trusting that things can improve or that we are worthy of love and success, more trust is placed in our inability to succeed or to find love.

Either way we look at it, full trust is being placed in something—so the question becomes, in which direction do we prefer to place our focus?

Releasing the mundane means cultivating the mindset that we do not need to grasp or gain anything outside of ourselves before we can feel whole and complete. A lot of us may have heard of this concept of wholeness before, but how many of us actually practice believing in it daily? How many of us continue to put more trust in the belief that we will attain happiness and peace as soon as we get a better job or a promotion, find a new partner or leave a current relationship, buy or pay off our house, get a better car, finish college, reach retirement, etc., etc., etc., ad infinitum? The challenge of this way of thinking is that there will always be something else to achieve right around the corner each time we accomplish a goal or reach a landmark. It's never ending, and so our search for happiness and peace also becomes unending.

Now that we have six tenets under our belts, Release the Mundane simply asks us to slow down and take pause. Easier said than done, yes, but by consistently practicing the other tenets with mindfulness, introspection, and meditation, we truly can stop feeding our ego in ways that keep us trapped in this cyclic pattern of setting goals, reaching them (or not), never finding lasting satisfaction, and repeating the process over and over again.

The difference between the blind and the wise is that the wise find gratitude and see worth in everything all the time, not just some of the time. They see worth in success and failure, they see worth in yesterday, in this moment, and in tomorrow. There is no separation (for they have transcended the duality) between what can bring happiness and peace and what cannot. Everything holds the seeds of awareness, and thus every experience is a fruit that can be enjoyed—even those that are sour! This fresh way of seeing the world we live in not only changes the way in which we relate to life, but it also transforms the way in which we relate to others and how we enjoy our relationships.

Nothing changes, and yet everything is different.

Understanding Trust:

Like birds, we have "wings", and having these "wings" releases our fear of falling because, even if the branch on which we rest breaks, we trust in our ability to fly.

Understanding Gratitude:

Each time we rejoice in the good fortune, blessings, and love we see others experiencing, it fosters good fortune, blessing, and love within ourselves.

Tenet Eight

Release Knowing

*To know is to first learn, then do.
The wise speak little for they are busy doing.
Justification and validation vanish;
The mind opens and wisdom is received.*

      Thought consumes energy. Talking and daydreaming about doing something is very different than actually going out and doing it—and yet, the brain rewards both, almost equally. Dopamine (the "feel good" hormone) is released when we think positively about doing something. It is also released when we actually go out and do it—and depending on what that something is, the mental high of what we romanticized can sometimes be more exciting than real life because others rarely meet our expectations.

      Dreams are bittersweet because we can get addicted to having ideas and talking about them, receiving gratification from others, yet never actually following through with the implementation. This is a cycle many people find themselves in; procrastinators raise your hands! Today's social media makes it easy for such dreamers to post about their workouts at the gym, their positive resolutions, their healthy diets, and to share "happy" photos of their relationships or friends—all the while feeling more alone than they ever have in their lives, binge-watching T.V. shows in the early morning hours of a sleepless night with fast-food wrappers crinkled up all around them.

      Release Knowing is all about bridging the gap between what we think and share and what we actually do. Without the applied awareness of this tenet, we become trapped in a prison made of our own ego-gratification, layering bricks of self-pity or pride (two sides of the same coin) ever higher and deeper. We receive just enough validation to get by without having to leave our comfort zone and fully transform ourselves.

One of the most common phrases heard in a life coach's, counselor's, or therapist's office (including my own) is, "I know". When people are being taught new material (or a new habit), the client, patient, or student tends to respond with those words. However! To know is to do, and what these individuals really mean to say is, "I am aware of this information, but I don't know how to effectively apply it." Therefore, it is of great benefit to simply scratch the phrase "I know" from our vocabularies; then we "know-it-alls" become "I-don't-know-at-alls" thus more teachable and ready to learn.

If, in fact, we replace all our "I knows" with "I don't know; please teach me"—we find this willingness does indeed have an impact on our mind's ability to receive vital information and pay attention because we are no longer subconsciously dismissing something we have heard before. And sometimes simply shifting our ability to read or hear something "old" into something to be experienced as "new" leads to a myriad of fresh insights that we have been missing due to the blindness or deafness our self-gratifying belief of "knowing" caused.

It's important to take this a step further. Awareness does not help us if we do not act upon said awareness. On our road toward inner peace, vulnerability is a must because, as shared in the second paragraph of this chapter, we project one image to the world while secretly living another way. Because of our attachments to our pride and our image, there is often a huge gap between our projected self and our authentic self.

Healing cannot occur until we become open to bridging this gap, and that is why vulnerability is necessary. We cannot heal what we do not acknowledge, and it takes a lot of courage to share a wound after being hurt. When a blossom opens, bees come to pollinate it, and the same applies when we open our hearts—we then gain the ability to receive love from others. When we finally reach the point of opening, all our justifying and need to validate ourselves comes to an end. This is a very humbling practice. We are then ready to listen, to receive, and to learn.

Remove your mask and give others the opportunity to love you for you.

Understanding Humility:

Humility is not only releasing arrogance and narcissism; it is also releasing self-pity and the need to degrade ourselves.

Understanding Vulnerability:

Vulnerability is being strong and secure enough to walk outside without your armor on.

Tenet Nine

Release Self

What is not acknowledged cannot be released.
To release self, one must understand oneself.
Love begins when peace is found,
Selfless service is achieved, then the cycle renews.

To release one's self, one must know oneself. Quite an interesting statement considering the previous tenet's focus on releasing knowing! However, as previously stated, we cannot heal what we do not acknowledge and embrace. Moving through each of the tenets provides us with the necessary insight to recognize our ego, our attachments, and our dualistic, discriminatory minds. By having a deep understanding of why we think and feel the way we do—and how much of it is actually ego-developed illusions that allow us to feel secure in a groundless world—we attain the initial stage of enlightenment. This means we become en-lightened, able to now see the conflict in the dark corners of our minds, our homes, our communities, and nations—all of it stemming from negative thought, irrational impulse, and emotional wounding.

Why do we place love last in this teaching? Because unconditional love only becomes possible when we achieve a state of inner peace. Otherwise, our love becomes the very reason for our suffering. We attach ourselves to the ones we love or we struggle with self-loathing (unable to love ourselves), both of which cause pain due to a false vision of human worth.

When we reach this place of peace, we have learned not to use other people, especially those we love, as an excuse for not feeling good. Love doesn't say, "It's because I love you that I'm upset!" Rather, love says, "It's because I love you that I am patient in my listening. I seek to understand where you are coming from." Taking this tenet even further, by releasing our "Self", or our collective perceived identities, we gain the ability to provide this unconditional love to all people—strangers and perceived foes alike. When we do not have a "Self", we cannot be insulted. Or rather, when we realize that our perceived "Self" is an illusory construct based on our ideas (and other people's ideas) of us, we cease to be offended and insulted, thus allowing ourselves to be fully present for others throughout the world. We become living, breathing embodiments of peace, inside and out.

On a final note, it is important to remember that inner peace and enlightenment is not a linear destination, rather, it is a way of life. The moment we cease speaking and behaving in the enlightened way of peace and compassion, the instant we fail to maintain a genuine desire to listen and understand—we lose our alignment. However far we swing away from our practice, that's the distance we can always swing back to regain it. This is why it is so necessary to maintain daily practice and self-discipline. The *Living Peace* teachings are not set forth as a ladder to climb and be done with each "rung" as we reach it; instead, they are set in a circle so that we continually revisit and relearn them. This Resurgence is the process that guides us back to Mastery of Thought, allowing the cycle to continue, but this time with full awareness of all the tenets. Even so, we remain open, and we find new insights in the teachings as we continue to learn how to apply each tenet simultaneously throughout the remainder of our daily lives.

Unconditional love is the outer expression of inner peace.

Understanding Love:

When we place peace before love, we realize that there is never a good enough reason to be out of alignment with peace.

Understanding Resurgence:

Instead of becoming enlightened beings, we become enlightened doers—there is no shortcut through or end to our daily peace practice.

Visit With Me

Study and train with me, Alaric, in person or long distance by visiting: www.EarthSpiritCenter.org

The expanded version of this introductory book is available on Amazon in print and as a digital download. *Living Peace* includes my personal—often humorous—anecdotes, in depth practices for each tenet, and additional teachings that expand upon the nine tenets, including the Five Layers of Consciousness.

Please share this book with friends and family, and even total strangers. I created this book with the intent to build bridges, which, if you have read this far, my intention is already being realized because a piece of my peace is now in your hands. Let these teachings also be a bridge for you, inviting conversations with others whom you normally might not talk to or might otherwise only speak to on a surface level. Everyone deserves a piece of peace. Our primarily roadblock to connecting more deeply with others prior to reading this book was that we simply did not know where to begin. Now we do.

www.ingramcontent.com/pod-product-compliance
Lightning Source LLC
Chambersburg PA
CBHW070042070426
42449CB00012BA/3144